TABLE OF CONTENTS

HOW IT WORKS

What are Popar® books?

Popar® books use Augmented Reality (AR) technology to create an immersive reading experience that will allow the user to see their books come alive with incredible, virtually "real" 3D objects, animations, and interactions that will pop off the page. Popar® books are designed to change the way we interact and experience stories, adventures, and learning.

What is Augmented Reality?

Our Augmented Reality (AR) is a ground breaking concept that uses a mobile/smart device and special patterns to make amazing and engaging 3D objects, animations, and interactions appear in the real world that maintain interest in all Popar® book series.

What do I need to see AR?

-Mobile/smart device that meets the minimum system requirements:

Apple® - iPhone® 4 or newer, iPad® 2 or newer, iOS 7 or above

Android™ - Smartphone or tablet w/ rear facing camera, ARM capable processor, Google Play™, OS 4.3 or above, (may not work on all Android™ devices)

-Included Popar® book app

-Popar® book

---

1 FIND

Use Mobile/Smart Device

Minimum requirements: Apple® iPhone® 4 or newer, or Apple® iPad® 2 or newer, iOS 7 or above. Android™ smartphone or tablet with a rear facing camera, ARM capable processor, and Google Play™ running OS 4.3 or above (may not work on all Android™ devices) to activate the Augmented Reality and other technology.

2 DOWNLOAD

Download the FREE App

Apple® users use the App Store and Android™ users use Google Play™. Search for **"Popar Sea Life 3D"**

3 EXPLORE

Look For Special ◉ Symbols

These symbols will show you where there are Augmented Reality (AR) interactions, videos, read-alongs, and games!

4 PLAY

Focus Your Mobile/Smart Device

Focus your mobile/smart device **24.5 cm** away from the special Augmented Reality (AR) symbols and watch the magic happen.

FEATURES FIND THIS

All Popar® books are packed full of fun, exciting, educational, and interactive features. As you learn and play with each action packed page, make sure you are keeping your eye out for the above special AR symbols. These symbols will show you where there is immersive Augmented Reality content waiting to be explored. Make sure to read the below instructions so you can learn more about the amazing 3D features that await exploration.

INTERACT

When you find one of the special AR symbols, you can interact with the 3D objects or animations simply with hand gestures on your mobile/smart device.

Touch
You can learn more information simply by touching the animation or object on your screen.

Swipe
You can also spin each object or animation by using your finger to swipe the screen.

Pinch
Enlarge or shrink the size of the 3D object or animation by pinching or expanding two fingers on your screen.

READ-ALONG

Every Popar® book has an educational read-along feature. Simply locate one of the special AR symbols on every page, and touch the AR enhanced area on the screen in order for the book to read to you. This feature is great for auditory learners. Learning and playing has never been so easy.

VIDEO

Popar® books are also filled with amazing educational videos that appeal to visual learners. When you find that special AR symbol, be prepared because you are in the front seat of the movie theatre as you get an up close and personal video experience.

Sharks are highly adapted predators, and they use their senses to hunt for prey. Great White Sharks are the largest predatory fish in the ocean. They can swim at speeds that exceed 56 km/h.

Sight

Sharks use their excellent sense of vision while hunting. Right up until the last second before a bite, they roll their eyeballs back into their head to prevent damaging them.

Smell

If a shark was put into a large swimming pool, it would be able to smell a single drop of blood in the water. In fact, two-thirds of a sharks brain is devoted to smell.

Hearing

Sharks have outstanding hearing. They can hear a fish thrashing in the water from as far as 243 m away. That is more than two football fields!

Touch
250 m

Hearing
500 m

Smell
4.8 km

Sharks are cartilaginous fish; that means their skeletons are made of cartilage with not a single bone in its body. Cartilage is flexible tissue that makes up human ears and noses.

A Great White's teeth can measure more than 5.7 cm long. They have five rows of 46 teeth each. At any one given time, there is an average total of 230 teeth. The teeth are arranged in rows like a conveyor belt, so when a tooth falls out from the front, the tooth from the next row moves up to take its place. This means Great White Sharks can have 50,000 teeth in a lifetime!

A female Great White will typically give birth to 8 or 9 pups. At birth, the baby shark is already about 1.5 m long, and grows to be three times that! Immediately after birth, the baby shark swims away from its mother before she has a chance to eat it. Baby sharks are on their own right away!

Shark attacks on humans are rare; most attacks on humans have occurred in the waters of the United States.

Great White
SHARK

In some regions, Great Whites have developed a hunting trick called a breaching attack. This is one of the most spectacular sights in nature.

When the shark sees its prey swimming above, the enormous force of the impact can lift even a big shark clean out of the water.

Size: 3.4 m to 6.4 m
Weight: 680 kg to 1,102 kg

4

Bottlenose Dolphins received their name because their beak is shaped like a bottle.

Bottlenose Dolphins look like they might be grinning. Their smiles are formed by the way their mouths curve.

BOTTLENOSE
DOLPHIN

Bottlenose Dolphins make a unique sound. Many of the sounds they make could be imitated by holding a balloon tightly by the neck, then letting the air out faster and slower.

Dolphins produce high frequency clicks that act as a sonar system called "echolocation" (ek-oh-low-KAY-shun). When the clicking sounds hit an object in the water, like a fish or rock, they bounce off and come back to the dolphin as echoes. Echolocation tells the dolphin the shape, size, speed, distance, and location of the object.

Dolphins also use body language to communicate including leaping as high as 6 m in the air; snapping their jaws; slapping their tails on the surface of the water; and even butting heads. They do this to alert each other to possible dangers, to let others know there is food nearby, and to keep track of others in the group. Nasal sacs inside the dolphin's head are responsible for allowing the dolphins to vocalise. Blowholes located behind their heads open and close, allowing the dolphins to breathe.

Size: 2 m to 4 m
Weight: 150 kg to 649 kg

6

CLOWN
Anemonefish

The clownfish, also known as a anemonefish, shares an amazing partnership with another sea creature, the anemone (uh-NEM-uh-NEE). The partnership benefits both participants, and the close relationship led to the fish being named an anemonefish.

Living among the tentacles of the anemone, the clownfish gains protection from predators that do not dare get near the stinging protector. The clownfish also gets to eat leftovers from the anemone's meals.

When clownfish hatch, they are all male. Under certain conditions, a male will change into a female but cannot change back. A clownfish only changes into a female to become the dominate female in a group. For instance, if a dominant female leaves or dies, the largest male in the group will change to become the breeding female.

Clownfish can survive the tentacle stings because of the layer of mucus on its skin that provides immunity to the anemone's stings.

In addition to anemone leftovers, they eat algae and plankton, tiny plants, and animals that float in the sea.

pufferfish

The pufferfish, also known as a blowfish, can fill its elastic stomach with huge amounts of water (sometimes air) in order to blow themselves up to several times their normal size.

SLOW

In order to escape predators, the pufferfish uses its unique defence mechanism to compensate for its slow locomotion.

Size: 2.5 cm to 61 cm
Weight: 4.1 kg to 13.6 kg

If the first line of defence does not deter a predator, all pufferfish species have pointed spines, shaping it into an uncomfortable, pointy ball and a possible choking hazard.

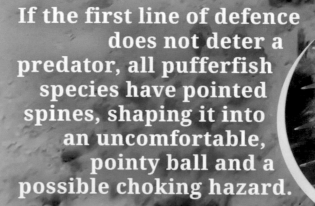

Most pufferfish contain a tetrodotoxin that makes them foul tasting and potentially deadly to other fish. The toxin is also deadly to humans. There is enough poison in one pufferfish to kill 30 adult humans, and there is no known antidote!

Pufferfish are scaleless fish and usually have rough or spiky skin.

Pufferfish are in the family "Tetraodontidae," which means "four teeth." Their teeth are fused together and are used to crush its prey.

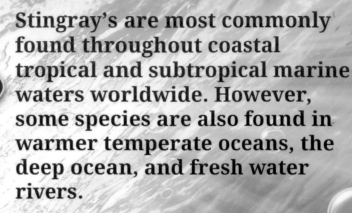

Stingray's are most commonly found throughout coastal tropical and subtropical marine waters worldwide. However, some species are also found in warmer temperate oceans, the deep ocean, and fresh water rivers.

Stingray

While the stingray's eyes peer out from its dorsal side; its mouth, nostrils, and gill slits are situated on its underbelly. The eyes are therefore not thought by scientists to play a considerable role in hunting.

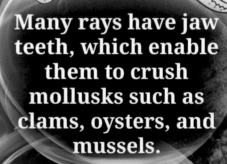

Many rays have jaw teeth, which enable them to crush mollusks such as clams, oysters, and mussels.

Size: .3 m to 4.6 m
Weight: .5 kg to 340 kg

The main predators of stingrays are: sharks, seals, sea lions, large species of carnivorous fish, and even humans.

The stingray's tail, otherwise known as its spine or barb, has serrated edges and a sharp point. The underside may produce venom that can be fatal to humans, and can remain deadly even after the stingray's death.

CAUTION
WATCH FOR STING RAYS
SHUFFLE YOUR FEET

Stingrays use their stinger to pierce through and stop its prey before it can escape.

Stingrays are also able to use their flattened body shape to their advantage by resting on the sea floor to hide from predators, as well as to keep an eye out for potential prey.

The stingray has electrical sensors called "Ampullae of Lorenzini." Located around the stingray's mouth, these organs sense the natural, electrical charges of potential prey.

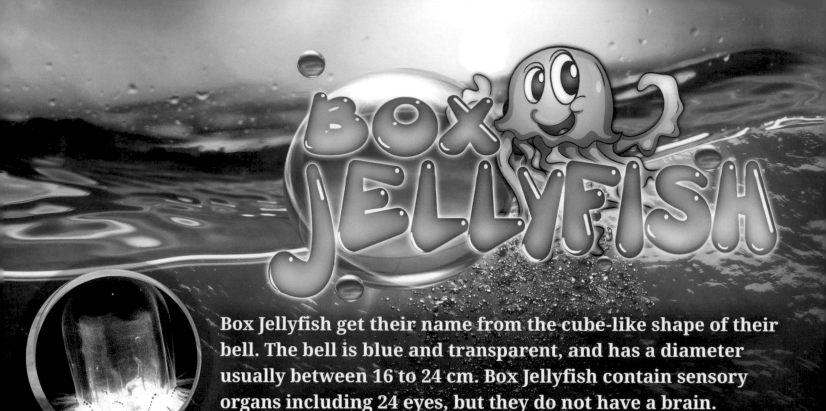

BOX JELLYFISH

Box Jellyfish get their name from the cube-like shape of their bell. The bell is blue and transparent, and has a diameter usually between 16 to 24 cm. Box Jellyfish contain sensory organs including 24 eyes, but they do not have a brain.

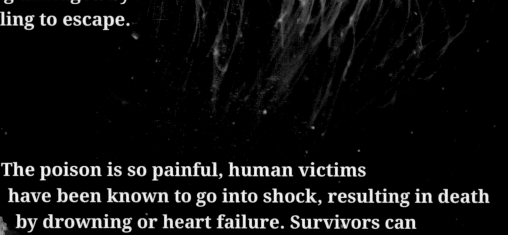

The Box Jellyfish developed its powerful venom to instantly stun or kill prey such as fish and shrimp. This prevented their delicate tentacles from being damaged by prey struggling to escape.

The poison is so painful, human victims have been known to go into shock, resulting in death by drowning or heart failure. Survivors can experience considerable pain for weeks, and often have scarring where the tentacles made contact.

Sea turtles are unaffected by the sting of the Box Jellyfish, and regularly eat them.

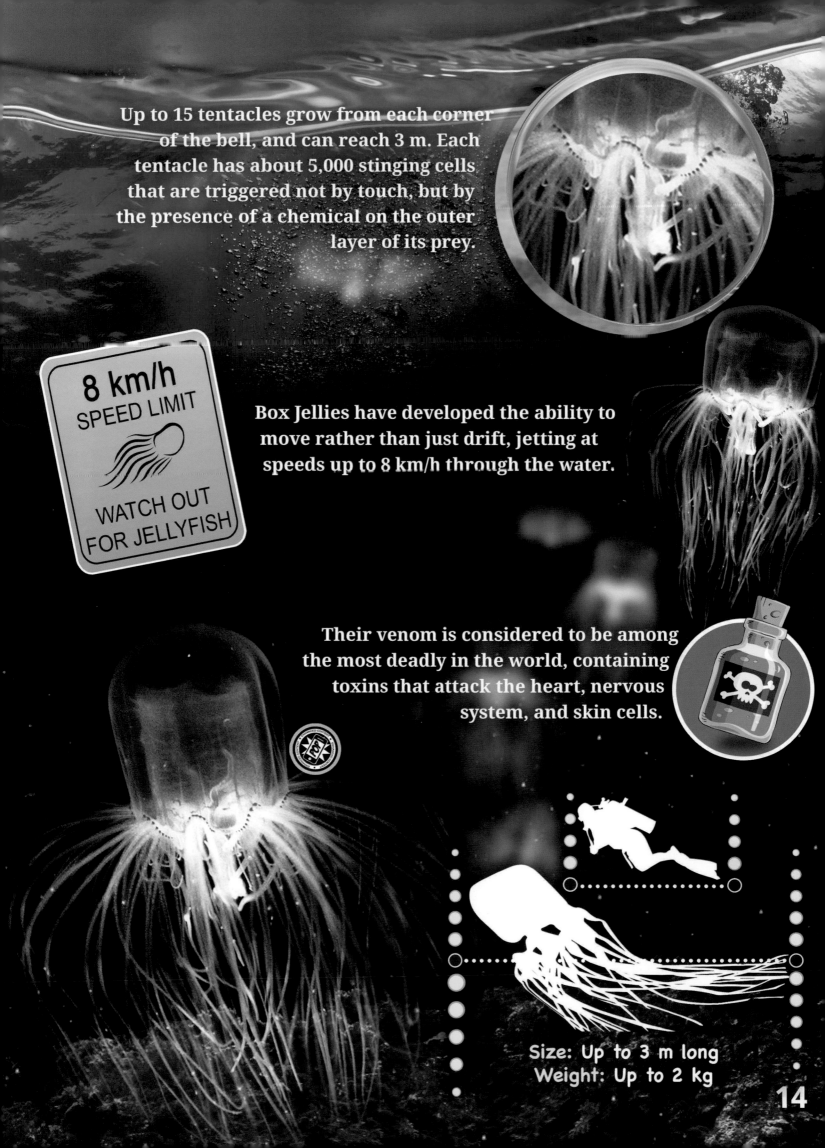

Up to 15 tentacles grow from each corner of the bell, and can reach 3 m. Each tentacle has about 5,000 stinging cells that are triggered not by touch, but by the presence of a chemical on the outer layer of its prey.

8 km/h
SPEED LIMIT

WATCH OUT
FOR JELLYFISH

Box Jellies have developed the ability to move rather than just drift, jetting at speeds up to 8 km/h through the water.

Their venom is considered to be among the most deadly in the world, containing toxins that attack the heart, nervous system, and skin cells.

Size: Up to 3 m long
Weight: Up to 2 kg

GIANT OCTOPUS

A female octopus lays thousands of transparent eggs under rocks or in holes. She guards the eggs for a period of four to eight weeks. When octopus hatch, they will drift along the ocean's surface for several weeks, where many are eaten by fish and other animals. Bottom-dwelling octopuses that survive this period, descend to live near the ocean's bottom.

Size: 3 m to 4.9 m
Weight: 10 kg to 45 kg

If an octopus loses an arm - no problem - a new one will grow back in its place!

An octopus can change into several different colours in order to blend in with its environment such as: grey, pink, brown, blue, or green. They also may change colour as a way to communicate with other octopus.

An octopus will typically drop down on its prey from above. They use their powerful suctions that line their arms, to pull their prey into their mouth.

Octopus are often considered "monsters of the deep," though some species occupy shallow waters. Most octopus stay along the ocean's floor in deep, dark waters, rising from below at dawn and dusk in search of food.

An octopus swims by blasting water through a muscular tube on their body called a siphon. When they crawl along the ocean's floor, they tuck their arms into small openings in search of food.

LOGGERHEAD SEA TURTLE

The Loggerhead is a beautifully coloured sea turtle that gets its name from its oversized head that looks like a big log. Loggerhead sea turtles live in the water, but they must surface to breathe.

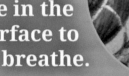

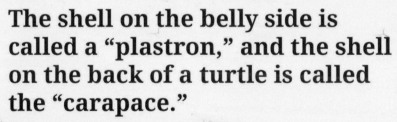

The shell on the belly side is called a "plastron," and the shell on the back of a turtle is called the "carapace."

The Loggerhead turtle population has been declining due to pollution, fishing nets, predators, and human development in their nesting areas, keeping this turtle on the threatened species list since 1978!

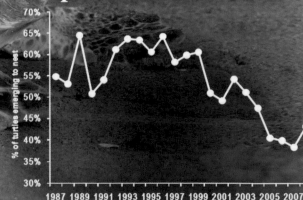

Laws prohibit people from harming Loggerheads and other sea turtles. Loggerheads frequently get tangled in fishing nets and drown, so laws require certain nets to have a device that allows sea turtles to escape if they get caught. These devices are called "turtle excluder devices."

Even in the buried nest, the Loggerhead eggs may fall prey to hungry raccoons or wild pigs that dig them up. The eggs that remain undisturbed, hatch about 60 days after being laid. Hatchlings dig their way up through the sand toward the surface, and wait just underneath the last layer of sand until nightfall to make their way to the ocean.

Size: 71 cm to 94 cm
Weight: 82 kg to 200 kg

A Loggerhead female generally nests every two to three years. After mating, she heads to shore to lay her eggs. On average, she will lay eggs four times in one nesting season. Each time, she comes ashore and uses her front flippers to clear a spot in dry sand. Then she uses her hind flippers to dig her nesting hole. She positions herself so that her eggs fall gently into the hole as she lays them.

18

SeaHorse

Seahorses are tiny fish that earned their name because their head looks like that of a tiny horse.

Seahorses have no teeth and no stomach. Food passes through their digestive system so quickly, they must eat almost constantly to stay alive! They graze continually and can consume 3,000 or more brine shrimp per day.

The male seahorse is equipped with a pouch on the front-side of its tail. During mating, the female seahorse can place as many as 1,500 eggs into the male's pouch. The male carries the eggs for 9 to 45 days until the seahorses are fully developed. Then the baby seahorses, each about the size of a small candy, float around in groups clinging to each other by their tails.

Seahorses anchor themselves with their prehensile tails to sea grass and coral, using their elongated snouts to suck in plankton and small crustaceans that drift by.

There are 54 species of seahorse that fall into the genus *Hippocampus*. They are found in the world's tropical and temperate coastal waters.

The seahorse can move its eyes independently of each other; that is helpful when keeping an eye out for predators.

Seahorses use their dorsal fins to propel through the water.

To move up and down, seahorses adjust the volume of air in pockets inside their bodies called "swim bladders."

Size: 1.5 cm to 35.5 cm
Weight: .2 kg to .5 kg

Tiny, spiny plates cover their bodies all the way down to their curled, flexible tails. The tail can grasp objects, and this is helpful when seahorses want to anchor themselves to vegetation.

Killer Whale

ORCA

The orca, commonly known as a "killer whale," is found throughout a wide range of the world's cold and tropical oceans. A typical orca bears a very distinctive black back, white chest and sides, and a white patch above and behind the eye. They have a great sense of hearing, stellar eyesight above and below the water, and a good sense of touch. Similar to dolphins, they also have sophisticated echolocation abilities.

Orcas hunt everything from fish, to walruses, seals, sea lions, penguins, squid, sea turtles, sharks, and even other kinds of whales. Depending on the season and where they are located, their diet varies; some orcas eat more fish and squid, than seals and penguins. But wherever they are in any of the world's oceans, average-sized orcas may eat about 227 kg of food a day. Orcas have many hunting techniques, and bumping seals off ice is just one of them.

Another unique hunting tactic, involves the slapping of an orca's tail on the water's surface in order to cause waves. These waves are intended to knock nearby prey such as penguins or sea lions off ice flows, and into the water where an orca is eagerly waiting.

Often referred to as wolves of the sea, orcas live and hunt together in cooperative pods, or family groups, much like a pack of wolves. They will work together to herd fish, or larger animals such as a blue whale, into a compact area so that they are easier to catch.

Size: 4.9 m to 9.8 m
Weight: 2,721 kg to 9,072 kg

Digital Toys Here

1 Cut out Popar® paddles on pages 24 and 26

2 Play with Popar® paddles

NEED HELP? GO TO WWW.POPARTOYS.COM FOR TECH SUPPORT.

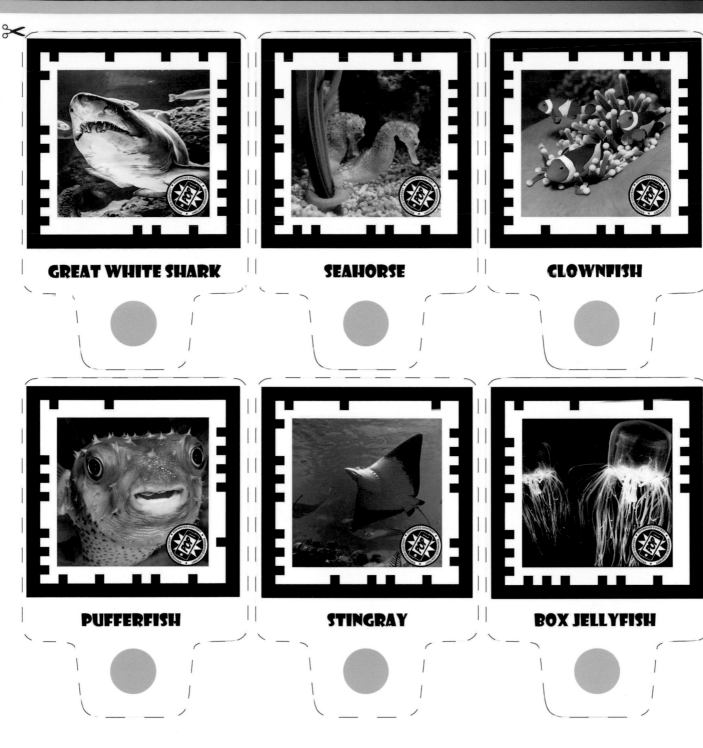

GREAT WHITE SHARK

SEAHORSE

CLOWNFISH

PUFFERFISH

STINGRAY

BOX JELLYFISH

Cut out or photocopy the Popar® paddles on this page. Use these paddles with a mobile/smart device and the FREE Popar® app when you are not reading the book. The Popar® paddles have the same amazing 3D objects, just like in the book. These 3D digital toys are great to play with and to take photos to share with your friends and family!

www.PoparToys.com

www.PoparToys.com

www.PoparToys.com

www.PoparToys.com

www.PoparToys.com

www.PoparToys.com